"Learn 15 Proven Strategies For Making Money On Youtube"

Introduction

Welcome to "15 Proven Strategies For Making Money On YouTube," an ebook designed to help you monetize your YouTube channel and turn your passion for creating videos into a profitable business.

YouTube has revolutionized the way people consume and share information, and it has also opened up new opportunities for content creators to earn money online. With over two billion active monthly users and over a billion hours of video watched every day, YouTube is the world's largest video-sharing platform.

However, making money on YouTube is not easy, and it requires dedication, hard work, and a deep understanding of the platform's monetization features. In this ebook, we will cover ten proven strategies for making money on YouTube, including advertising revenue, sponsorships, merchandise sales, and more.

Whether you're a beginner or an experienced YouTuber, this ebook will provide you with practical tips and strategies to help you grow your channel, engage with your audience, and make money online. We will cover everything from setting up your YouTube channel to creating high-quality content, promoting your videos, and optimizing your monetization strategy.

So, if you're ready to turn your YouTube channel into a profitable business, let's dive into the ten proven strategies for making money on YouTube!

Index

- Sponsorships
- Merchandise sales
- Affiliate marketing
- Channel memberships
- Super Chat and Super Stickers
- Crowdfunding
- YouTube Premium revenue
- Live events
- Brand deals
- Licensing your content
- Consulting services
- Writing a book
- Selling courses
- Creating apps or software

Chapter 1

Advertising revenue: This is the most common way to earn money on YouTube. Once you join the YouTube Partner Program (YPP), you can earn

money from ads displayed on your videos

Advertising revenue is the most common way for YouTubers to make money from their channels. It works by displaying ads on their videos and paying them a share of the revenue generated from those ads. In this section, we will provide a complete summary of how advertising revenue works on YouTube.

Firstly, to monetize your videos on YouTube, you need to join the YouTube Partner Program (YPP). The program is available to channels that meet certain eligibility criteria, such as having at least 1,000 subscribers and 4,000 watch hours in the past 12 months. Once you join the YPP, you can start monetizing your videos through advertising revenue.

The next step is to enable monetization on your videos. This can be done by going to your Video Manager and selecting "Monetization" for each individual video. You can also enable monetization for all your videos at once by going to your Channel Settings and selecting "Monetization."

Once you have enabled monetization, YouTube will start displaying ads on your videos. The type of ads that are displayed depends on the advertiser's preferences and the viewer's location, interests, and browsing history. There are several types of ads, including display ads, overlay ads, skippable video ads, non-skippable video ads, bumper ads, and sponsored cards.

When a viewer clicks on an ad or watches it for a certain amount of time, the advertiser is charged for the ad. YouTube then shares a portion of that revenue with the video creator. The exact percentage that YouTube pays varies depending on several factors, such as the type of ad and the location of the viewer. In general, the revenue share is around 55% for the video creator and 45% for YouTube.

It's important to note that not all videos are eligible for monetization. YouTube has strict guidelines on what content can be monetized, and it's essential to follow those guidelines to avoid having your monetization revoked or your channel terminated. Some of the things that can affect your eligibility include copyright infringement, graphic or violent content, and hateful or harmful content.

To maximize your advertising revenue, it's essential to create high-quality content that engages your audience and keeps them watching for as long as possible. The longer viewers watch your videos, the more ads they will see, and the more revenue you will earn. It's also important to promote your videos on social media, collaborate with other YouTubers, and use keywords and tags that are relevant to your content.

In summary, advertising revenue is a popular way for YouTubers to make money from their channels. By enabling monetization and following YouTube's guidelines, you can display ads on your videos and earn a share of the revenue generated from those ads. To maximize your revenue, it's important to create high-quality content and engage with your audience to keep them watching for as long as possible.

Chapter 2

Sponsorships: Brands are always looking for influencers to promote their products. If you have a large following, you can work with brands to create sponsored content

Sponsorships are a popular way for YouTubers to make money by collaborating with brands and promoting their products to their audience. In this section, we will provide a complete summary of how sponsorships work on YouTube. Firstly, to get sponsorships, you need to have a sizeable and engaged audience. Brands are looking for influencers who can promote their products to a large and relevant audience. You also need to have a niche that aligns with the brand's products or services. For example, if you have a cooking channel, a kitchen appliance brand might be interested in sponsoring your content.

The next step is to approach brands that you want to work with. You can reach out to them directly, or you can use platforms that connect influencers with brands, such as FameBit or Grapevine. It's essential to have a clear and professional pitch that outlines what you can offer to the brand, such as the number of subscribers, engagement rates, and demographics of your audience.

Once you have agreed on the terms of the sponsorship, you need to create content that promotes the brand's products or services. This can be done in several ways, such as creating a dedicated video, including a sponsored message in your video, or featuring the product in your video. It's important to disclose that the content is sponsored and to follow YouTube's guidelines on advertising disclosures.

The compensation for sponsorships varies depending on the brand and the type of content. Some brands pay a flat fee for a sponsored video, while others pay based on the number of views or conversions that the content generates. It's essential to negotiate the terms of the sponsorship and ensure that you are being compensated fairly for your time and effort.

To maximize the effectiveness of sponsorships, it's essential to choose brands that align with your values and niche. You should also create content that is authentic and engaging, and that showcases the brand's products or services in a positive light. It's important to be transparent with your audience and to only promote products that you believe in.

It's also essential to comply with YouTube's guidelines on advertising disclosures. You should clearly disclose that the content is sponsored in the video and in the video description. Failure to comply with these guidelines can result in the revocation of your monetization or termination of your channel.

In summary, sponsorships are a popular way for YouTubers to make money by collaborating with brands and promoting their products to their audience. By having a sizeable and engaged audience, approaching brands directly or through platforms, and creating authentic and engaging content, you can earn a fair compensation for your time and effort. It's important to choose brands that align with your values and niche, to comply with YouTube's guidelines on advertising disclosures, and to create content that showcases the brand's products or services in a positive light.

Chapter 3

Merchandise sales: You can sell your own branded merchandise, such as t-shirts or mugs, through your YouTube channel

Merchandise sales are a popular way for YouTubers to make money by selling their own branded merchandise to their audience. In this section, we will provide a complete summary of how merchandise sales work on YouTube.

The first step is to create a design for your merchandise that aligns with your brand and appeals to your audience. You can use platforms such as Teespring or Merch by Amazon to create and sell your merchandise, or you can use a third-party print-on-demand service. It's important to choose high-quality materials for your merchandise and to ensure that the design is clear and appealing.

Once you have created your merchandise, you need to promote it to your audience. You can do this by creating a dedicated video or social media post that showcases your merchandise and encourages your audience to purchase it. You can also include links to your merchandise in your video descriptions and social media bios.

The compensation for merchandise sales varies depending on the platform and the type of merchandise. Some platforms pay a flat fee for each item sold, while others pay a percentage of the sale price. It's essential to research the different platforms and choose the one that offers the best compensation and the most benefits.

To maximize the effectiveness of merchandise sales, it's essential to create merchandise that aligns with your brand

and niche. You should also promote your merchandise in a way that is engaging and authentic, and that encourages your audience to support your brand. It's important to provide high-quality customer service and to respond to any questions or concerns that your customers may have.

It's also essential to comply with YouTube's guidelines on advertising disclosures. If you promote your merchandise in a video, you should disclose that the content is sponsored in the video and in the video description. Failure to comply with these guidelines can result in the revocation of your monetization or termination of your channel.

In summary, merchandise sales are a popular way for YouTubers to make money by selling their own branded merchandise to their audience. By creating high-quality and appealing merchandise, promoting it in an engaging and authentic way, and providing excellent customer service, you can earn a fair compensation for your time and effort. It's important to choose a platform that offers the best compensation and benefits, to create merchandise that aligns with your brand and niche, and to comply with YouTube's guidelines on advertising disclosures.

Chapter 4
Affiliate marketing: You can earn a commission by promoting other people's products or services through affiliate marketing. For example, you can include affiliate links in your video descriptions

Affiliate marketing is a popular way for YouTubers to make money by promoting products and services to their audience and earning a commission on any resulting sales. In this section, we will provide a complete summary of how affiliate marketing works on YouTube.

The first step is to join an affiliate program that offers products or services that align with your niche and audience.

Some popular affiliate programs include Amazon Associates, eBay Partner Network, and Commission Junction. Once you have joined an affiliate program, you can access a unique tracking link that identifies you as the affiliate and tracks any resulting sales.

Next, you need to promote the products or services to your audience. This can be done in several ways, such as creating a dedicated video that showcases the product or service, including a sponsored message in your video, or featuring the product or service in your video. It's important to disclose that the content is sponsored and to follow YouTube's guidelines on advertising disclosures.

The compensation for affiliate marketing varies depending on the program and the type of product or service. Most programs offer a percentage of the sale price as a commission, which can range from a few percent to over 50%. It's essential to choose affiliate programs that offer a fair commission and products or services that align with your values and niche.

To maximize the effectiveness of affiliate marketing, it's essential to choose products or services that align with your niche and audience. You should also create content that is authentic and engaging, and that showcases the product or service in a positive light. It's important to be transparent with your audience and to only promote products or services that you believe in.

It's also essential to comply with YouTube's guidelines on advertising disclosures. You should clearly disclose that the content is sponsored in the video and in the video description. Failure to comply with these guidelines can result in the revocation of your monetization or termination of your channel.

In summary, affiliate marketing is a popular way for YouTubers to make money by promoting products and services to their audience and earning a commission on any resulting sales. By joining affiliate programs that offer products or services that align with your niche and audience, promoting the products or services in an engaging and authentic way, and complying with YouTube's guidelines on advertising disclosures, you can earn a fair compensation for your time and effort. It's important to choose affiliate programs that offer a fair commission and products or services that align with your values and niche, and to create content that showcases the product or service in a positive light.

Chapter 5

Channel memberships: Once you have 30,000 subscribers, you can offer channel memberships to your audience. This allows them to access exclusive content and perks in exchange for a monthly fee

Channel membership is a feature on YouTube that allows viewers to support their favourite creators by paying a monthly fee in exchange for exclusive perks and benefits. In this section, we will provide a complete summary of how channel membership works on YouTube.

To be eligible for channel membership, your channel must have at least 30,000 subscribers and be a member of the YouTube Partner Program. Once you meet these requirements, you can apply for channel membership and set up the perks and benefits that you will offer to your members.

The perks and benefits that you offer to your members can include exclusive access to your community posts, live chats, and emojis, early access to your videos, shoutouts, and personalised messages. You can set the monthly fee that your members will pay, and you will receive a portion of the fee as revenue.

To promote your channel membership to your audience, you can create a dedicated video that explains the benefits and encourages viewers to sign up. You can also include links to your membership page in your video descriptions and community posts, and promote it in your social media channels.

The compensation for channel membership varies depending on the number of members and the monthly fee. You will receive a portion of the monthly fee as revenue, and this will be paid out to you on a monthly basis. It's essential to offer perks and benefits that are valuable to your members and to provide excellent customer service to your members.

To maximize the effectiveness of channel membership, it's essential to create perks and benefits that align with your brand and audience. You should also promote your channel membership in an engaging and authentic way, and that encourages your audience to support your channel. It's important to provide high-quality customer service and to respond to any questions or concerns that your members may have.

It's also essential to comply with YouTube's guidelines on advertising disclosures. If you promote your channel membership in a video, you should disclose that the content is sponsored in the video and in the video description. Failure to comply with these guidelines can result in the revocation of your monetization or termination of your channel.

In summary, channel membership is a feature on YouTube that allows viewers to support their favourite creators by paying a monthly fee in exchange for exclusive perks and benefits. By setting up valuable and engaging perks and benefits, promoting them to your audience in an authentic and engaging way, and providing excellent customer service to your members, you can earn a fair compensation for your time and effort. It's important to comply with YouTube's guidelines on advertising disclosures, to provide high-quality customer service, and to create perks and benefits that align with your brand and audience.

Chapter 6

Super Chat and Super Stickers: These features allow your viewers to pay to have their messages highlighted in the chat during a livestream

Super Chat and Super Stickers are two features on YouTube that allow viewers to support their favourite creators during live streams and premieres. In this section, we will provide a complete summary of how Super Chat and Super Stickers work on YouTube.

Super Chat allows viewers to purchase a highlighted message that appears in the live chat during a live stream or premiere. The message is highlighted in a bright colour, making it stand out from the rest of the chat. The amount of the purchase determines the duration of time the message stays pinned to the top of the chat, with higher amounts resulting in a longer duration. Creators can also choose to pin the Super Chat message to their channel feed after the live stream or premiere has ended.

Super Stickers are animated images that viewers can purchase during live streams and premieres. There are a variety of sticker options to choose from, such as a thumbs up, a bouncing ball, or a cute animal, and the price of each sticker varies depending on the design.

To use Super Chat and Super Stickers, viewers must have a valid payment method linked to their Google account. They can then select the Super Chat or Super Sticker option and choose the amount they wish to spend. The Super Chat or Super Sticker message will then appear in the live chat, with the duration or animation depending on the amount spent.

Creators receive a portion of the revenue generated from Super Chat and Super Stickers, and they can see a summary of their earnings in their YouTube analytics dashboard. The revenue is paid out on a monthly basis, and creators can use the funds to support their channels or invest in new content.

To maximise the effectiveness of Super Chat and Super Stickers, it's important to encourage viewers to use the features and to provide engaging and interactive content during live streams and premieres. Creators can also offer exclusive perks and benefits to Super Chat and Super Sticker users, such as shoutouts, personalised messages, or early access to content.

It's important to comply with YouTube's policies and guidelines when using Super Chat and Super Stickers. This includes not promoting inappropriate or harmful content, not using the features to artificially inflate view counts or engagement, and not engaging in fraudulent activity.

In summary, Super Chat and Super Stickers are features on YouTube that allow viewers to support their favourite creators during live streams and premieres. By providing engaging and interactive content and offering exclusive perks and benefits, creators can encourage viewers to use the features and earn a fair compensation for their time and effort. It's important to comply with YouTube's policies and guidelines and to use the features in an ethical and transparent way.

Chapter 7

Crowdfunding: You can use crowdfunding platforms, such as Patreon or Kickstarter, to ask your audience to support your channel financially

Crowdfunding is a method of raising money for a project or business by soliciting small contributions from a large number of people, typically via the internet. In this section, we will provide a complete summary of how crowdfunding works on YouTube.

YouTube creators can use crowdfunding platforms such as Patreon, Kickstarter, and Indiegogo to raise funds from their viewers and fans. Creators can set up a page on these platforms and offer rewards or benefits to supporters who contribute to their campaign. These rewards can include exclusive content, merchandise, early access to videos, or personalised messages.

To maximise the effectiveness of a crowdfunding campaign, creators should have a clear and compelling message that resonates with their audience. They should also set realistic fundraising goals and offer enticing rewards to encourage viewers to contribute. Regular updates and engagement with supporters can help to maintain momentum and build a sense of community around the project.

There are several types of crowdfunding available on these platforms, including:

Donation-based crowdfunding: Supporters donate money to a project or cause without expecting anything in return.

Reward-based crowdfunding: Supporters contribute money in exchange for a reward or benefit, such as exclusive content, merchandise, or personalised messages.

Equity-based crowdfunding: Investors contribute money in exchange for a share of the project or business's ownership.

Debt-based crowdfunding: Investors contribute money in exchange for a fixed return on investment.

Creators can choose the type of crowdfunding that best suits their needs and goals.

Crowdfunding can be a useful way for creators to generate revenue for their channels and fund new projects or initiatives. However, it's important to comply with the policies and guidelines of the crowdfunding platform and to be transparent and honest with supporters. Creators should also ensure that they have the necessary permissions and licences to undertake their project or business, and that they have a clear plan for how the funds will be used.

In addition to crowdfunding platforms, YouTube has its own crowdfunding feature called "YouTube Memberships." This feature allows viewers to support their favourite creators by becoming a channel member and paying a monthly fee in exchange for exclusive perks and benefits, such as badges, emojis, and access to members-only content. Creators can set their own monthly membership fees and offer different tiers of membership with varying benefits.

To maximise the effectiveness of YouTube Memberships, creators should offer unique and valuable perks that are not available to non-members. They should also promote the feature to their viewers and provide regular updates and engagement with their members.

In summary, crowdfunding is a method of raising money for a project or business by soliciting small contributions from a large number of people. YouTube creators can use crowdfunding platforms such as Patreon, Kickstarter, and Indiegogo to fund their channels and new projects, and can offer rewards or benefits to supporters in exchange for their contributions. Creators should comply with the policies and guidelines of the crowdfunding platform and be transparent and honest with supporters. YouTube also has its own crowdfunding feature called "YouTube Memberships," which allows viewers to support their favourite creators and receive exclusive perks and benefits.

Chapter 8

YouTube Premium revenue: You can earn a share of the revenue generated by YouTube Premium subscribers who watch your content

YouTube Premium is a subscription service that allows users to watch videos on YouTube without ads, access exclusive content, and download videos for offline viewing. In this section, we will provide a complete summary of how YouTube Premium revenue works for creators.

Creators who have content on YouTube may earn revenue from YouTube Premium subscribers who watch their videos. When a YouTube Premium subscriber watches a video from a creator, a portion of their subscription fee is distributed to the creator as part of the YouTube Premium revenue share. The revenue share is based on the amount of time that YouTube Premium subscribers spend watching a creator's videos. This means that creators who have high-quality, engaging content that keeps viewers engaged for longer periods of time may earn more revenue from YouTube Premium.

YouTube Premium revenue is calculated based on a formula that takes into account the total watch time of YouTube Premium subscribers on a creator's videos as a percentage of the total watch time of all YouTube videos by YouTube Premium subscribers. The revenue share varies based on factors such as the number of YouTube Premium subscribers who watch a creator's videos and the total amount of watch time generated by those subscribers.

It's worth noting that the amount of revenue earned from YouTube Premium can vary depending on the country where the content is being viewed. Revenue from YouTube Premium may also fluctuate based on changes in the number of YouTube Premium subscribers or the amount of watch time generated by those subscribers.

To maximise the potential revenue from YouTube Premium, creators should focus on creating high-quality, engaging content that keeps viewers engaged for longer periods of time. They can also promote the benefits of YouTube Premium to their viewers and encourage them to subscribe to the service.

In addition to earning revenue from YouTube Premium, creators who have exclusive content may also be able to earn additional revenue by making that content available to YouTube Premium subscribers. This can be done through YouTube's Originals program, which allows creators to produce and distribute exclusive content on the platform.

In summary, YouTube Premium is a subscription service that allows users to watch videos on YouTube without ads, access exclusive content, and download videos for offline viewing. Creators who have content on YouTube may earn revenue from YouTube Premium subscribers who watch their videos. The revenue share is based on the amount of time that YouTube Premium subscribers spend watching a creator's videos. To maximise the potential revenue from YouTube Premium, creators should focus on creating high-quality, engaging content that keeps viewers engaged for longer periods of time, and promote the benefits of YouTube

Premium to their viewers. Creators who have exclusive content may also be able to earn additional revenue through YouTube's Originals program.

Chapter 9

Live events: You can organize live events, such as meet-and-greets or concerts, and sell tickets to your audience

Live events are a great way for YouTube creators to engage with their audiences and generate additional revenue. In this section, we will provide a complete summary of how live events work on YouTube and how creators can monetize them.

YouTube Live is a feature that allows creators to broadcast live video content to their audience in real-time. Live events on YouTube can be anything from Q&A sessions, product launches, concerts, and other performances.

Creators can monetize their live events on YouTube in several ways. The first way is through advertising revenue. YouTube inserts ads in the live stream and creators earn a percentage of the ad revenue generated during the stream. In addition, creators can also use Super Chat and Super Stickers during their live streams to earn additional revenue. Super Chat and Super Stickers are features that allow viewers to make a monetary contribution to the creator during the live stream.

Another way to monetize live events on YouTube is through sponsorships. Creators can partner with brands and companies to promote their products or services during the live event. This can be done through product placement, sponsor mentions, or other forms of advertising. Sponsors may also provide financial support for the event, which can help cover the costs of production and increase the revenue generated by the event.

Creators can also use live events as an opportunity to promote and sell merchandise. They can create exclusive products or offer limited edition merchandise during the live event to generate additional revenue. This can be a great way to increase the engagement of their audience and promote their brand.

Live events can also be used as a way to generate revenue through ticket sales. Creators can sell tickets to the live event or offer exclusive access to the event to their Patreon supporters. This can be a great way to generate additional revenue and provide exclusive content to their most dedicated fans.

YouTube creators can also use live events as a way to increase their audience engagement and build their community. Live events provide a unique opportunity for creators to interact with their audience in real-time and build stronger connections with their fans.

In summary, live events on YouTube provide creators with a unique opportunity to engage with their audience and generate additional revenue. Creators can monetize their live events through advertising revenue, sponsorships, merchandise sales, ticket sales, and other forms of monetization. Live events can also be used as a way to increase audience engagement and build a strong community. With the right approach and planning, YouTube live events can be a powerful tool for creators to grow their channels and increase their revenue.

Chapter 10

Brand deals: You can work with brands to create custom content or sponsor your videos

Brand deals are a popular way for YouTube creators to monetize their channels and earn income. In this section, we will provide a complete summary of how brand deals work on YouTube and how creators can maximize their earnings through partnerships with brands.

A brand deal is an agreement between a YouTube creator and a brand or company. The brand pays the creator to create content that promotes their product or service. This can take many forms, including sponsored videos, product placement, sponsored social media posts, and other types of content.

Brand deals can be a lucrative source of income for creators, but it's important to approach them carefully to ensure that they align with the creator's brand and values. A successful brand deal should benefit both the creator and the brand, providing value to the creator's audience while also promoting the brand's product or service.

To find brand deals, creators can reach out to brands directly or work with a third-party agency or network that specializes in influencer marketing. These agencies can connect creators with brands that are a good fit for their channel and negotiate deals on their behalf.

When creating sponsored content, it's important for creators to disclose that the content is sponsored. This can be done in a variety of ways, such as by adding a disclaimer in the video description, using the hashtag #ad or #sponsored, or stating at the beginning of the video that it is sponsored content.

One key factor that brands look for when partnering with creators is audience reach and engagement. Brands want to work with creators who have a loyal and engaged audience that is likely to be interested in their product or service. Creators can increase their chances of landing brand deals by growing their audience and engagement through consistent, high-quality content and active social media presence.

When negotiating brand deals, creators should consider the amount of work involved in creating the content and the value of their time and audience. They should also consider how the brand deal fits into their overall content strategy and whether it aligns with their values and brand identity.

In summary, brand deals can be a valuable source of income for YouTube creators, but it's important to approach them carefully and strategically. Creators should focus on building a loyal and engaged audience and working with brands that align with their values and brand identity. By creating high-quality, sponsored content that benefits both the creator and the brand, creators can maximize their earnings and build long-term partnerships with brands that will benefit their channel in the long run.

Chapter 11

Licensing your content: You can license your videos to other platforms or media companies for a fee

Licensing your content is another way for YouTube creators to monetize their channel and earn income. In this section, we will provide a complete summary of how content licensing works on YouTube and how creators can maximize their earnings through licensing agreements.

Licensing your content means allowing others to use your videos for their own purposes in exchange for a fee. This can include licensing your content for use in television shows, commercials, movies, or other types of media. Creators can also license their content to brands or companies for use in their advertising campaigns or promotional materials.

To license your content, creators can work with licensing agencies or distribution companies that specialize in securing licensing deals. These companies will help to promote your content to potential clients and negotiate licensing agreements on your behalf. Creators can also license their content directly by listing their videos on stock footage websites or other online marketplaces.

When licensing your content, it's important to have a clear understanding of the terms and conditions of the licensing agreement. Creators should ensure that the terms of the agreement are fair and that they are compensated appropriately for the use of their content. This may include negotiating the length of the licensing agreement, the types of media in which the content can be used, and the amount of compensation that the creator will receive.

To maximize their earnings through licensing, creators can focus on creating high-quality, visually stunning content that is in high demand. This may include videos of scenic locations, wildlife, or other subjects that are popular among brands, advertisers, and media companies. Creators can also consider creating unique and innovative content that stands out from the crowd and has a high potential for licensing.

It's also important for creators to have a solid understanding of copyright laws and to ensure that they have the rights to license their content. Creators should ensure that they have the appropriate licenses for any music, images, or other materials that appear in their videos and that they are not infringing on the rights of others.

One potential drawback of licensing your content is that it may limit your control over how your content is used. Creators should be aware that once their content is licensed, they may not have control over how it is edited, re-purposed, or distributed. Creators should also be aware that licensing their content may affect their ability to monetize their content through other channels, such as advertising revenue or merchandise sales.

In summary, licensing your content can be a valuable source of income for YouTube creators, but it's important to approach it carefully and strategically. Creators should work with reputable licensing agencies or distribution companies, ensure that they have the appropriate licenses for their content, and negotiate fair and reasonable terms for their licensing agreements. By creating high-quality and visually stunning content, creators can maximize their earnings and build a sustainable income stream through licensing their content.

Chapter 12
Consulting services: If you have expertise in a certain area, you can

offer consulting services to your audience

Consulting services can be a profitable way for YouTube creators to earn income by leveraging their expertise and knowledge. In this section, we will provide a complete summary of how consulting services work on YouTube and how creators can offer their services to clients.

Consulting services involve providing expert advice and guidance to clients on a specific topic or area of expertise. YouTube creators can offer consulting services to clients who are interested in learning more about a particular topic, or who need help with a specific project or challenge. Consulting services can be offered in a variety of formats, including one-on-one coaching, group workshops, online courses, or through email or phone consultations.

To offer consulting services on YouTube, creators should first identify their area of expertise and determine the type of services they can offer. Creators can then market their services through their YouTube channel by creating content that demonstrates their knowledge and expertise. This may include creating instructional videos, tutorials, or webinars that showcase their skills and expertise.

Creators can also create a separate website or landing page that provides more information about their consulting services and how clients can work with them. This may include a description of the services offered, pricing information, and testimonials from past clients.

When offering consulting services, it's important for creators to establish clear expectations with their clients, including the scope of the project, the timeline for completion, and the fees involved. Creators should also set boundaries for their availability and communicate these to their clients to avoid potential misunderstandings.

To maximise their earnings through consulting, creators can focus on building a strong reputation for their expertise and delivering high-quality services to their clients. Creators can also consider offering package deals or discounts for repeat clients, as well as creating additional services or products that complement their consulting services.

One potential drawback of consulting services is that it can be time-consuming and may take away from the time and resources needed to create content for their YouTube channel. Creators should also be aware of the potential liability risks involved in providing consulting services and take steps to protect themselves through appropriate legal agreements and insurance.

In summary, consulting services can be a valuable way for YouTube creators to monetise their knowledge and expertise, but it requires a strategic approach and careful planning. Creators should identify their area of expertise and determine the type of services they can offer, market their services through their YouTube channel and website, establish clear expectations with clients, and focus on building a strong reputation for their expertise. By delivering high-quality services and leveraging their knowledge and skills, creators can build a sustainable income stream through consulting services.

Chapter 13

Writing a book: If you have a lot of knowledge in your niche, you can write a book and promote it through your YouTube channel

Writing a book can be a profitable way for YouTube creators to leverage their expertise and build their brand. In this section, we will provide a complete summary of how writing a book works on YouTube and how creators can get started. Writing a book involves creating an original piece of work that shares insights, knowledge, or stories on a specific topic or area of expertise. YouTube creators can leverage their platform and audience to create a book that complements their brand and provides additional value to their followers. A book can help creators expand their reach and build credibility as an expert in their field.

To get started with writing a book, creators should first identify their area of expertise and determine the type of book they want to write. Creators can choose to write a non-fiction book that shares insights or advice on a specific topic, or a memoir that tells a personal story. Creators can also choose to self-publish their book or seek a traditional publishing deal.

Once the book is written, creators can market their book to their YouTube audience by creating promotional content, such as book trailers, author interviews, or readings. Creators can also leverage their social media platforms to reach a wider audience and promote their book.

To maximise their earnings through writing a book, creators can focus on building a strong marketing plan, securing media coverage, and creating additional products or services that complement their book. Creators can also consider hosting book signings or speaking engagements to promote their book and engage with their audience.

One potential drawback of writing a book is that it can be time-consuming and may take away from the time and resources needed to create content for their YouTube channel. Creators should also be aware of the potential costs involved in self-publishing or seeking a publishing deal, as well as the potential risks of copyright infringement or plagiarism.

In summary, writing a book can be a valuable way for YouTube creators to monetise their expertise and build their brand, but it requires careful planning and execution. Creators should identify their area of expertise and determine the type of book they want to write, market their book to their YouTube audience, and focus on building a strong marketing plan to maximise their earnings. By creating a high-quality book and leveraging their platform and audience, creators can build a sustainable income stream through writing.

Chapter 14

Selling courses: You can create and sell online courses that teach your audience a particular skill or topic

Selling courses is a popular way for YouTube creators to monetise their expertise and provide additional value to their audience. In this section, we will provide a complete summary of how selling courses works on YouTube and how creators can get started.

Selling courses involves creating and selling an online educational program that shares insights, knowledge, or skills on a specific topic or area of expertise. YouTube creators can leverage their platform and audience to create a course that complements their brand and provides additional value to their followers. A course can help creators expand their reach and build credibility as an expert in their field.

To get started with selling courses, creators should first identify their area of expertise and determine the type of course they want to create. Creators can choose to create a video course that is hosted on a platform like Udemy, Skillshare, or Teachable, or they can create a course that is hosted on their own website.

Creators can create a course using a variety of formats, including pre-recorded videos, live webinars, PDFs, or interactive modules. The course should be engaging and provide actionable insights or skills that learners can use to improve their lives or businesses.

Once the course is created, creators can market their course to their YouTube audience by creating promotional content, such as course trailers, instructor interviews, or previews of course content. Creators can also leverage their social media platforms to reach a wider audience and promote their course.

To maximise their earnings through selling courses, creators can focus on building a strong marketing plan, securing media coverage, and creating additional products or services that complement their course. Creators can also consider offering a money-back guarantee or offering a free trial period to entice potential learners.

One potential drawback of selling courses is that it can be time-consuming and may take away from the time and resources needed to create content for their YouTube channel. Creators should also be aware of the potential costs involved in creating a course, such as hosting fees, software costs, or marketing expenses.

In summary, selling courses can be a valuable way for YouTube creators to monetise their expertise and provide additional value to their audience, but it requires careful planning and execution. Creators should identify their area of expertise and determine the type of course they want to create, market their course to their YouTube audience, and focus on building a strong marketing plan to maximise their earnings. By creating a high-quality course and leveraging their platform and audience, creators can build a sustainable income stream through selling courses.

Chapter 15

Creating apps or software: If you have programming skills, you can create apps or software that are relevant to your niche and sell them to your audience

Creating apps or software is another way for YouTube creators to monetize their expertise and provide additional value to their audience. In this section, we will provide a complete summary of how creating apps or software works on YouTube and how creators can get started.

Creating an app or software involves developing a program that provides a solution or service to a specific problem or need. YouTube creators can leverage their platform and audience to create an app or software that complements their brand and provides additional value to their followers. An app or software can help creators expand their reach, build credibility, and provide an additional income stream.

To get started with creating an app or software, creators should first identify a problem or need within their niche that their audience faces. Creators can choose to develop an app or software on their own or partner with a developer to bring their idea to life.

Creators can create an app or software that solves a problem, enhances the user experience of their content, or provides additional resources to their audience. An app or software can be designed for various platforms, including iOS, Android, or desktop.

Once the app or software is created, creators can market their product to their YouTube audience by creating promotional content, such as product demos, tutorials, or previews of the app or software's features. Creators can also leverage their social media platforms to reach a wider audience and promote their app or software.

To maximize their earnings through creating apps or software, creators can focus on building a strong marketing plan, securing media coverage, and creating additional products or services that complement their app or software. Creators can also consider offering a free or lite version of their app or software with the option for users to upgrade to a paid version with more features.

One potential drawback of creating apps or software is that it can be time-consuming and require technical expertise. Creators should also be aware of the potential costs involved in creating an app or software, such as development fees, software costs, or marketing expenses.

In summary, creating apps or software can be a valuable way for YouTube creators to monetize their expertise and provide additional value to their audience, but it requires careful planning and execution. Creators should identify a problem or need within their niche, develop an app or software that complements their brand, and focus on building a strong marketing plan to maximize their earnings. By creating a high-quality app or software and leveraging their platform and audience, creators can build a sustainable income stream through creating apps or software.